COOKERY FOR NORTHERN WIVES

COOKERY

FOR

NORTHERN WIVES

COMPILED FOR

HOME AND SCHOOL

BY

MARGARET B. STOUT

Diplomee of the Edinburgh School of Cookery.

CONTAINING PRACTICAL RECIPES FOR OLD-TIME AND
MODERN DISHES, ALL SUITED TO THE
HIGHLANDS AND ISLANDS OF
SCOTLAND.

This edition is a facsimile version of the original published by:

T. & J. MANSON, LERWICK

1925

Reprint 2013

T. & J. MANSON, *Shetland News* OFFICE, LERWICK

MARGARET BANNATYNE STOUT
1894–1982

MARGARET STOUT was born in Lerwick in 1894, the fifth child of Charles Brown Stout, Chemist and Master Druggist, and Margaret Mainland Stout, of the Medical Hall, Lerwick.   She attended, as did her seven brothers and sisters, the Anderson Institute and excelled as a performer in dramatic productions and recitations, many written in the Shetland dialect.

In 1915 Margaret Stout graduated from the Edinburgh School of Cookery and Domestic Economy with a First Class Diploma.   The First World War was still raging in Europe.   She promptly applied her newly gained qualifications to the war effort, lecturing and writing on War Time Cookery in Shetland and Scotland.   She was appointed to her first teaching post in London, and supervised a canteen on King's Cross Station in the early morning and evening for Scottish Troops returning to France.   She was awarded the Red Triangle for her two years war service.

Margaret Stout returned to Shetland in 1921 and it was then that she decided to gather material for a Shetland Cook Book. She had two aims, to encourage young northern wives to cook simple, inexpensive and wholesome dishes, and secondly to research and record traditional Shetland recipes which had evolved by rule of thumb and passed from mother to daughter. She tested all the recipes in the old kitchen of the Medical Hall. The freshly slaughtered carcass of a lamb was essential to demonstrate that traditionally every part of the lamb was used, so she prudently took the maid, who was from the country, with her to the auction of sheep and lambs at the Market Green in Lerwick. They bought a lamb for 6d. The maid walked the lamb to the slaughter house and returned to the Medical Hall with the carcass.

Cookery for Northern Wives was published by T. & J. Manson in 1925. Margaret Stout travelled the world returning to Scotland in the late 1920s, where she became Area Organiser for the Scottish Woman's Rural Institutes. She was based in Aberdeen but made frequent visits to Shetland to form new institutes. Margaret Stout later returned to Shetland to teach Domestic Science in Lerwick, and continued to research and record traditional Shetland crafts. She taught night classes in hand dying and hand spinning Shetland wool, and designing and making Shetland Taatit rugs.

In 1935 she was awarded the Gold Star at the National Woman's Rural Institute's Exhibition in London for a model of a Shetland Woman dressed authentically in traditional costume.

During the Second World War the Island women, always resourceful, turned to their native dishes and the first edition of Cookery for Northern Wives completely sold out! Miss Stout, now Mrs Dennis, gave talks on War Time Cookery and Make Do and

Mend.   She hated food waste and would have given her full support to the green food agenda.

This facsimile of the first edition of Cookery for Northern Wives retains the spirit of the original work. In 1965 a second and revised cdition of the book, now titled The Shetland Cookery Book, was published and ran to three editions.   The preface by Marion McNeill, the Scottish food historian and author, has been included in this facsimile, as well as the original foreword by Jessie M.E. Saxby.

I would like to think that my mother's Shetland Cookery Book, which is part of our heritage, will have a place in the Shetland Book collection.

MARGARET STUART.

FOREWORD.

WOMEN of the Shetland Isles have a genius for cooking. A few lessons will render our lasses excellent cooks, but small opportunity is theirs for learning the art. The ordinary cookery books deal chiefly with dishes whose ingredients are usually beyond the reach of our cottagers. In past times the fish kettle, broth-pot and frying-pan were about all the utensils they possessed. Their crofts supplied them with potatoes, cabbage and turnip; but no one showed them how to grow variety of vegetables. Fruit they had none. Butcher meat was seldom obtainable. Groceries were meagre in variety and uncertain in supply. Yet they managed to turn out wholesome, if plain meals.

Even now that supplies can be counted upon, and American stoves, with good coal, take the place of the peat-fire on the hearth, there is need for lessons on Cookery to take the place of "rule of thumb." This brochure meets the Shetlander's requirements. It does not profess to deal with dishes beyond simple ones whose ingredients are within reach. The recipes are clearly and intelligently "set out." The old time cookery ought still to be in force, and this little book will teach many a Shetland girl to compound dishes popular in her grandmother's time. The local terms, and names of dishes will interest a wide circle of readers beyond our Isles.

Miss Margaret Stout's Cookery College training in Edinburgh, and her intimate acquaintance with the domestic life of her compatriots, entitle her booklet to be one of the very best authorities on the subject. Let us hope that its pages will cause many of our "mate-midders" to set aside the tinned meats so commonly used now and revert to the wholesome food of their forbears.

JESSIE M. E. SAXBY.

PREFACE

Today, the nations of the world are drawing closer together in amity, and that is all to the good; but at the same time each nation should take care to preserve its distinctive customs and traditions in order to avoid subsiding into a drab uniformity. Part of our enjoyment in travelling abroad lies in sampling the various national and regional dishes of the countries we visit, and each country should preserve these dishes as part of its heritage.

It is a truism that the people who have lived longest in a particular region know best how to use the products of that region. Food redolent of the soil and sea retains something valuable that is lost in freezing, canning and processing generally—what has been called "the subtle elements of freshness". So, however sophisticated and internationally-minded we become in the affairs of the kitchen, let us be careful to preserve those regional dishes that have been handed down by rule-of-thumb for countless generations.

It is just this that Margaret Stout has done for her native islands. After obtaining her diploma at a well-known School of Cookery, she returned

to Shetland and set about collecting the recipes
for those dishes that composed the traditional
diet of the Shetlanders and had produced a hardy,
energetic and intelligent race. They were
published (many of them for the first time) in
1925, under the title, COOKERY FOR NORTHERN
WIVES.

A personal note: It happens that I was born
in Shetland's twin archipelago, Orkney, and as
Miss Stout suggests, it is highly probable that
in our youth we sometimes sailed together, un-
wittingly, on the Orkney and Shetland steamer
to Leith, whence she proceeded to the Edinburgh
School of Cookery and I to the University of
Glasgow. As a fellow-Isleswoman and fellow-
enthusiast for folk-cookery, it gives me great
pleasure to introduce and warmly recommend
this revised edition of her book.

F. MARION McNEILL.

AUTHOR'S NOTE.

THIS little book is published with the earnest hope that it may serve a double purpose : that of diffusing the knowledge required for the preparation of simple and wholesome dishes and of awakening interest in the manifold uses to which our forbears put every particle of foodstuff available. These were "lean" days in the eyes of the present generation, inasmuch as our ancestors did not have the variety of articles of diet that are to be purchased in our northern land to-day. Nevertheless out of the native fish, flesh, fowl and grain, generation after generation of housewives evolved such a wide variety of dishes that there was no suspicion of leanness there in the eyes of the contented folk who knew not the allurements of our imported eatables, provided that the year was a fruitful one. Time has wrought a complete change in our dietary, in some ways for the worse, in others for the better. If the imported foodstuffs are used judiciously they add much to our store of health and enjoyment; if used to excess or if ill-cooked they are detrimental to health.   It is all, naturally, a matter of intelligence.

"COOKERY FOR NORTHERN WIVES" does not aim at being, in any sense, a complete cookery book, however small.   There are dozens of such books on the market, each excellent in its way.   The aim has rather been to gather together the recipes peculiar to Shetland, Orkney and the North of Scotland which have been evolved by a rule of thumb method and passed on from mother to daughter with varying degrees of exactness, and to rewrite them with some thought of scientific proportion.   These recipes are in danger of passing away with the present generation because, with the facility of modern transit, foodstuffs from the south are being more and more generally used to the exclusion of the native produce.   Land that once grew the native grains now provide pasture for animals.   In many ways the change, though inevitable, is to be regretted, for there is no doubt that a hardy race with good teeth, muscle and bone thrived upon the food used langsyne.

We would not wish to return completely to the old way of living as regards eatables.   A judicious combination of the old and new should give the best results and suit our peculiar climate and natural conditions.   To this end a number of recipes have been included which were entirely unknown to our ancestors but the ingredients of which can now be purchased in the most remote outposts of our land.

Certain mysterious elements of food called *vitamines* are much talked of to-day by dietitians, although their nature and action are as yet the subjects of experiment. Their presence controls growth and other bodily functions, and they are found in varying proportion in different foodstuffs. Cod liver oil for instance has been shown to contain a very much larger proportion of a certain vitamine than butter fat or vegetable fat. Bere or barley meal similarly is vastly richer than wheat. This is to be remembered when there is an opportunity to make a good dish of "stap" or some beremeal bannocks, and it serves to explain why our people have been the hardy race they were and to warn us that too great a change in our dietary may result in an enfeebled generation. "Native food for native folk" should be heard more often, especially when it is remembered that as a rule it is cheapest and generally best.

In conclusion, I would remind our readers that certain Shetland dishes were always eaten on certain days long ago, although of course eaten also on other days throughout the year. For instance, on Beainer

Sunday (Sunday before Christmas) it was usual to hang up an ox head in the chimney to make broth with; on Jöl E'en or Christmas Eve virpa (sowans) invariably formed the supper. On Christmas Day itself breakfast was the main meal at which all kinds of meat available, except pork, were served; stovies formed a popular dish on that occasion. Fastern's E'en, a moveable feast, had to have a supper of brose and half a cow's head. On Bogl Day, about the end of March, (commencement of delving) a supper was served consisting principally of cakes named " bogles," one for each member of the family On Lammas Sunday, milgruel was served for breakfast; next day the meadows were begun to be mown. " Bride's Bonn " appeared at weddings, and so on. These customs are practically dead now, but they are interesting reminders of the esteem in which certain native dishes were held.

The author's sincere and grateful thanks are due to a number of friends who have helped with suggestions and recipes, especially to her father and mother, the latter having a wonderfully complete knowledge of and interest in the food of our people.

MARGARET B. STOUT.

CONTENTS.

HANDY MEASURES.

1 Teacupful Sugar	...	...	...	6 oz.
1 Teacupful Flour	...	...	...	4 oz.
1 Teacupful Cheese	...	...	...	3 oz.
1 Teacupful Breadcrumbs		...	...	2 oz.
1 Tablespoonful Flour	...	...	...	1 oz.
1 Dessertspoonful Flour		...	...	$\frac{1}{2}$ oz.
1 Teaspoonful Flour	...	...	...	$\frac{1}{4}$ oz.
1 Dessertspoonful Butter, etc.	...		...	1 oz.
1 Tablespoonful Syrup or Treacle		...	2 oz.
1 Teacupful Liquid	...	...	...	1 gill.
1 Breakfastcupful Liquid		...	...	$\frac{1}{2}$ pint.

NOTE.—A " spoonful " means as much above the bowl of the spoon as is in the bowl of the spoon—*i.e.,* a " heaped " spoonful .

ERRATUM.

———

Page 27, line 8—For " *Note.* —If liver is large, use a little more flour,"

read—

"*Note.* —In certain districts when milk was "

EXPLANATION OF TERMS.

TO SCALD—Pour on boiling water and pour off again.

TO BLANCH—Put on with cold water, bring to boil and pour water away.

TO CREAM—Mix thoroughly together to a creamy consistency.

DICE—Small squares about $\frac{1}{4}$ inch.

TO BREAK DOWN—The blending of a dry ingredient with a liquid, gradually, to prevent lumps.

STIFF PASTE—A mixture which leaves the basin clean.

SOFT PASTE—A mixture which drops easily from the spoon.

BATTER—A mixture of flour and a liquid thin enough to pour.

TO BROWN—To fry lightly in smoking hot fat until a dark brown colour.

TO SIMMER—Only bubbling at one side of the pan.

FISH IN SEASON (NORTH OF SCOTLAND).

NOTE.—The months named are inclusive.

FISH.	TIME.
COD	January to May.
FLOUNDER ...	December to May.
HADDOCK	December to February.
HAKE	June to August.
HALIBUT	March to May.
HERRING	Winter, January to February.
	Summer, 20th June to August.
HOE	June to August.
LING	January to May.
MEGRIM	March to May.
MACKEREL	As herring. Winter mackerel inferior to Summer mackerel.
NORWAY HADDOCK	Spring.
PLAICE	December to May.
SKATE	March to May.
SOLE	December to May.
SAITHE	June to August (best in August).
TURBOT	March to May.
TUSK	January to May.
TROUT	August.
WHITING	All year round. Plentiful in June and July. Spawn any time.

COOKERY FOR NORTHERN WIVES.

Fish.

In Shetland fish is generally bought in larger quantities than in the cities; usually one has to arrange fish on the menu according to the market, controlled by the weather. When good a large bunch may be bought at a very moderate cost, considering the food value, and the housewife is often perplexed as to how to utilize them to the best advantage and not cause the menu to be monotonous.

Choice.—The eyes should be bright and prominent, gills red, fresh smell, stiff, and well filled out.

If small fish be obtained, they may be fried, baked in batter, etc. Those not to be used immediately may be dried, sprinkled with salt and hung outside. If large fish, the heads and trimmings may be used for fish soup. One fish may be cut into neat fillets and prepared for frying for breakfast; another boiled and allowed to get cold, the fish removed from the bones, when it will keep for a few days to be used for fish pie, salad, fish cakes, etc.

To Prepare Fish for Cooking.—This is very often carelessly done and detracts exceedingly from the dish.

B

Wash thoroughly in cold water, scale from the tail to the head, holding knife flat against the fish.   Remove all black skin and blood, especially the clot of blood half way down the fish.   Do not handle more than necessary.   Remove eyes without breaking them; trim fish with scissors, removing fins, cut tail V shape. These trimmings are used for fish stock or sauce.

TO SALT FISH.

METHOD.

Clean the fish, dry well; make a pickle of salt and water strong enough to float a potato.   Allow the fish to soak in this for 24 hours, string up and hang outside until perfectly dry and salt is seen glistening on the outside.

TO PRESERVE FISH WITHOUT SALT.

Fish for home consumption was seldom salted but preserved in the three following ways :—

(1)   *Reested*—dried inside with fire and smoke.

(2)   *Blawn*—dried in the wind, called Stock-fish. This was apt to be insipid, therefore it was prepared for cooking in this way—beat with hammer until soft, soak in milk and warm water, well seasoned.

(3)   *Gozened*—dried in the sun.

SKRAEFISH.

This is fish dried in the sun without being salted.

FISH SOUP.

Trimmings and Head of Large Fish.
One Small Haddock.
Salt.   Six Peppercorns.
One Onion.
Cold Water to cover.

METHOD.

Thoroughly cleanse the trimmings, put into pan with cold water, salt, peppercorns and onion, bring slowly to boil, skim. Add seasonings, simmer for 40 minutes and strain.   Return to pan; break down 2 tablespoons flour to each quart of stock with a little milk, add to pan, bring to boil, season if necessary and serve.   The addition of chopped parsley is an improvement.

TO BOIL FISH.

If the fish is small, keep on the head, if large, cut into suitable sized pieces as large as possible. The aim in boiling fish is to cook it without breaking it. To ensure keeping the fish whole, tie in a piece of clean muslin or put inside two white paper bags and tie with string around; but if carefully boiled this is not necessary.   Allow 1 dessertspoonful salt and vinegar to each quart of water.

METHOD.

Put fish into boiling salted water, simmer gently until cooked.   Allow 5—10 minutes for small fish, and

10-15 minutes to the lb. for larger fish, but if thick allow longer time.   Drain well and serve with butter or sauce.

TO FRY FISH.

This is a good method to use for small fish, whitings, trout, etc.

METHOD.

Prepare as usual, dry well;   skin if desired from head to tail (except flat fish);   toss in flour to dry and enable batter to adhere.   Make a batter thick enough to just drop from spoon and coat the fish all over. Have ready a pan with enough fat, smoking hot, to come half way up the fish.   Fry a golden brown on both sides, drain well on clean white paper.   Serve very hot.

BOILED SALT FISH AND SAUCE.

One pound Salt Cod.
One ounce Flour.
One ounce Margarine.
Half a pint of Milk.
Pepper and Salt.
One Hardboiled Egg (chopped roughly).

METHOD.

Wash and trim fish, remove skin;   soak for 2—3 hours, or if very salt for longer, changing the water several times.   Put into pan of cold water (without salt) and bring to boil.   Boil for 20—30 minutes until tender;   drain and serve with sauce.

WHITE SAUCE.—Melt butter, add flour, mix well together;   add half milk, stir continually until it boils, beating out all lumps;   add rest of milk, bring to boil, season, add the egg.   Coat the fish neatly or serve sauce separately.

HERRING AND CABBAGE.

METHOD.

Boil a cabbage until tender, drain and chop.   Add a small pat of butter, a little pepper and stew gently for a few minutes.   Split open a red herring, toast before the fire, pick from the bones, mix thoroughly with cabbage and serve hot, forked up in a pie-dish.

FINNAN HADDOCKS.

METHOD.

(1) *GRILLED.*—Have ready a clear, red fire;   lay haddock on grill or on tongs across fire, grill first one side and then the other.   Rub with pat of butter and serve.   The haddock may also be toasted before the fire.   All the juices and flavour of the fish are retained.

(2) *STEWED.*—Wash fish and cut into neat pieces.   Put into pan with a little milk, water and pat of butter, season and stew gently for 10—15 minutes.

SKUED HADDOCKS.

Two Haddocks.   One Onion.
One ounce of Butter.
Pepper and Salt.
One tablespoonful of Flour.

METHOD.

Wash and skin the fish, lay in a pan with two cups of water, onion, butter and seasoning; simmer gently for 10—20 minutes (according to fish).   Add flour broken down with little milk or water, simmer another 10 minutes, dish and serve hot.

LIVER MUGGIES.

The muggie is the stomach of the fish, and the ling muggie is best for this dish.

METHOD.

Wash the muggie and tie the small end with string tightly.   Break up or slice the liver, season well and fill the muggie three-quarters full, thus leaving room for the shrinking of the muggie.   Tie tightly with string about one inch down so that the string does not slip off.   Plunge into boiling salted water and boil gently 25-30 minutes.   Remove from water, drain and serve hot with potatoes.   The muggie can now be eaten as well as the liver·

HAKKA MUGGIES.
METHOD.

Prepare as in Liver Muggie.   Fill up with liver,

oatmeal and seasoning alternately, about half a table-spoonful at a time until half to two-thirds full. Close, leaving room for oatmeal to swell, and cook as before. Cod, ling or tusk liver may be used for this dish.

Cod liver contains most oil, therefore is most suitable. Be sure that the liver is quite fresh before using; ling liver is generally to be depended on.

KRAPPIN MUGGIES.

METHOD.

Prepare a krappin mixture, half fill the muggie; close the end, boil or bake.

KRAPPIN.

One pound of Liver (or two cupfuls).
Quarter of a pound of Flour (one cupful).
Quarter of a pound of Beremeal or fine Oatmeal.
One teaspoonful of Salt.
Pepper.

METHOD.

Put all into a basin and with the hand thoroughly mix together, breaking down the liver until the mixture forms a ball and holds together. Thoroughly wash a fish head, remove blood and gills and stuff with mixture. Cook in boiling salted water for 20—30 minutes.

(2) Put mixture (as above) into clean dry white paper bag and put this inside another bag; tie around with string, plunge into boiling water and boil for half an hour.

Note.—If ling liver is used the mixture may become too soft; add a little more flour until of the proper consistency.

STAP.

Two Haddocks.
Two Haddock Livers.
Pepper and Salt.

METHOD.

Wash the livers, put into jam jar, cover with paper and set in pan of boiling water; cook for one hour. Wash, clean fish, cut in two or three and boil; drain and dish. Take one piece of fish, remove skin and bone and add to liver. Chop all together, season and dish in piedish neatly; serve with fish, piping hot.

LIVER KROLLS.

Four handfulls of Beremeal.
Pinch of Salt.
Cold Water to mix.
Small cup of Sillock Livers.

METHOD.

Mix the meal to a paste with water; form into a round cake with hollow in the centre. Fill with liver and seasoning; cook either in oven or on brand-iron.

This dish may also be made with any other meal mixed with water and a lump of butter; it is eaten either raw or cooked.

LIVER FLACKIES.

METHOD.

Take two half dried (suket) piltocks, split them and remove the rig.   Between them put fresh liver and bake on hearthstone or in oven 5—10 minutes.

COD SOONDS BROILED, WITH GRAVY.

METHOD.

Scald the soonds in hot water, rub over with salt and blanch.   Remove black skin, return to pan with cold water, bring to boil, and simmer till almost tender. Remove from pan, toss in seasoned flour and grill. Serve hot with white sauce or gravy around.

TO CRIMP COD, DUTCH STYLE.

METHOD.

Wash, clean and trim cod;   cut in slices $\frac{3}{4}$ to 1 inch thick.   Have a pan of very salted boiling water, boil for two minutes;   drain, toss in our and broil.

PROG.

This dish is similar to Stap.

METHOD.

Boil some piltocks, skin and bone them.   Flake the fish, put the livers into a pan and heat until they oil;   remove any sediment and mix well together.   Season well and serve hot.

LIVER CUIDS.

METHOD.

Clean the piltocks by making an insertion below the gills, try not to cut the stomach.   Wash the fish, remove tails.   Wash the livers, roll in salt and pepper; drop in about three livers in each piltock.   Close the opening either by filling up with crust of bread or by breaking away the gills at the top and bending them backwards and filling them into the opening.   Grill or bake the piltocks 5—10 minutes until cooked.   Serve very hot.   In the country districts these were generally roasted on a brandiron over glowing peat embers.

LIVER KRUS.

This is a cup made of dough, filled with livers and roasted on the hearth.

MOUGILDIN *OR* SPIOLKIN.

Piltocks or sillocks roasted with the livers inside them.

KRAMPIES.

Sillock Livers.
Burstin.

METHOD.

Wash the livers, put into an old pan or jam jar standing in a pan of water, until cooked.   Put the livers, very hot, into a basin and beat in enough warm burstin until all the liver is absorbed and the mixture is of a soft consistency. Season well and serve hot.

Note.—In Unst this used to be sometimes made with meal and refuse of tallow when rinding down fat.

LIVER KOOGS.

METHOD.

Wash several large potatoes. Cut off the top of each and remove a little potato from the centre. Fill with fish liver, season well with salt and pepper, replace the top. Bake among hot peat "brands" on the hearth until well cooked.

GREE'D FISH.

METHOD.

Boil the fish, drain and dish on ashet. Melt the liver until it oils, remove sediment if possible, or strain over fish; sprinkle with pepper and salt and serve hot.

LIVER HEADS.

METHOD.

Wash the head, keep in the gills, wash the livers and put inside head. Close the mouth by stitching; cook in boiling salted water three quarters of an hour, if a small head half an hour· Drain, lay on hot plate, quickly remove large bones, chop all together. Season, and serve very hot.

BRISMIK HEADS.

This is similar to Liver Heads, only tusk heads are used and are roasted either in oven or over hot peat embers.

KIOSSED HEADS.

These are small sillocks or heads rolled in a cloth and put into the crevice of a stone wall until they acquire a gamey flavour.   Then they are cooked, being generally roasted and eaten with butter and potatoes.

TURBOT HEAD ROASTED.

As there is a natural oil in the turbot no liver is required.   Season and roast in oven or on brandiron for about half an hour.   This makes an excellent dish.

TURBOT REEKLINS.

This is the flesh of halibut cut into strips and dried in peat smoke·

SLOT (1).

One Cod Roe.
One quarter of a Ling Liver.
One cupful of Flour.
Pepper and Salt.

METHOD.

Skin the roe, add liver and enough flour to bind;

beat well together until thoroughly mixed. Have ready
a pan of boiling fish "broe" or boiling salted water;
with a saucer dipped in hot water lift out a portion of
slot, drop into the boiling water and cook for 20—25
minutes.   The boiling water will cause a coating to
form on the outside of the slot and keep the portions
from breaking.   Serve very hot.

SLOT (2).

One Cod Roe.
Flour.   Seasoning.

METHOD.

Beat the roe to a cream;   add a little flour and
seasoning.   Roughly shape into balls and drop into
boiling salted water.   When cooked (20—25 minutes)
cool, slice and fry in butter or fat.   Serve hot.

NOTE—The recipe for Slot varies a great deal
according to the district.   As a rule the taste of the
liver should not be pronounced.   Sometimes more
flour was added, but the mixture must not be of too
stiff a consistency.   To get the correct saltness, a pan
consisting of half sea water and half fresh water was
generally used.   Sometimes the Slot was dropped into
a ladle in boiling water, and the ladle withdrawn after
it had formed shape.

BAKED TURBOT WITH ONIONS.

METHOD.

Wipe and trim the fish, lay in greased Yorkshire

tin with a spoonful of dripping on top and enough hot water to cover bottom of tin ; cover with greased paper. Bake in a moderate oven 40—50 minutes; when half done cover with two onions finely chopped, and continue cooking until finished.   Dish neatly with onions on top.

ROE CAKES.

Half a pound of Roe.
Half a teacupful of Flour.
One Egg.   Half a cup of Milk.
Pepper and Salt.
Quarter of a teaspoonful of Cream of Tartar.
Good pinch of Baking Soda, or
Half a teaspoonful of Baking Powder.

METHOD.

Boil the roe, allow to cool; skin and with the hands break up in a basin until there are no lumps.   Add dry ingredients and mix with spoon until the flour is thoroughly incorporated with roe.   Add beaten egg and milk, beat all well together.   Melt two tablespoonfuls dripping in a frying pan, allow to become smoking hot ; fry mixture in spoonfuls until a golden brown on both sides, about 5—7 minutes.   Add more dripping from time to time.   Drain and serve hot.

FRIED TUSK LIVERS ON TOAST.

METHOD.

Wash and dry the livers, sprinkle with pepper and salt.   Grease a frying pan, heat, fry the livers on both sides till brown and cooked.   Serve hot on fresh dry toast.

STUFFED AND BAKED HADDOCK.

One large Haddock.

STUFFING—

Four tablespoonfuls of Bread Crumbs.
Two tablespoonfuls of Chopped Suet.
Half a teaspoonful of Powdered Herbs.
Pepper and Salt.   One Egg.
Half a teaspoonful of Chopped Parsley.

METHOD.

Prepare stuffing; mix ingredients together and bind with beaten egg, keeping back a little.   (Substitute—little milk and flour).   Prepare fish as usual, dry, fill with stuffing, brush over with remainder of beaten egg and coat with dried crumbs.   Melt 2 tablespoonfuls dripping in a tin and bake fish in a moderately hot oven 20-30 minutes, basting occasionally.   Dish neatly, pour around anchovy sauce (white sauce with anchovy essence seasoning).

Note.—A slice of cod may be baked in same way, Remove bone carefully, make half the stuffing, place in centre, piling high; tie string around outside of cut to keep from breaking; cook as before.

BAKED FISH IN BATTER.

This is especially suitable for small fish, *i.e.,* whitings, which become soft when boiled and difficult to dish.

Three Whitings.   Four ounces of Flour.
Salt and Pepper.
Quarter of a teaspoonful of Baking Soda.
Quarter of a teaspoonful of Cream of Tartar.
Half a pint of Milk.

METHOD.

Prepare fish, cut in two; lay in Yorkshire tin in which two tablespoons of dripping have been melted. Make a smooth batter, pour over fish, bake in a moderate oven 20-30 minutes till fish is cooked and batter brown.

FRESH HERRINGS.

Fresh herrings are excellent if cleaned, scaled and fried.   As they contain a large percentage of fat in the form of oil, very little fat is required for frying.   As many people object to fried herring on account of the indigestibility of the fat, this may be remedied by baking in vinegar and water, which counteracts the fattiness.

BAKED HERRINGS.

METHOD.

Remove heads, split down front, remove bones by holding fish with head towards one, and working thumb under the bones to carefully loosen them out to end of " wings."   Sprinkle with salt and pepper, roll up from tail to head, place in tin or piedish with enough water and vinegar to almost cover.   Bake in a moderate oven for $\frac{3}{4}$ hour, dish and strain liquid over them.

SALT HERRINGS.

HERRING SALAD.

Five medium-sized Onions.
Three Herrings.
Twelve Peppercorns.
Pepper and Salt.
Vinegar to cover.

METHOD.

Wash, skin and clean herring thoroughly.   Remove bones from head downwards, split open from back and cut in 8 or 10 pieces.   Lay in piedish with alternate layers of onion, add seasonings, cover with vinegar and allow to stand overnight.   The salad is ready for use next day.   The vinegar softens the bones and the salad will have all the appearance and taste of cooked herring.   The addition of boiled sliced beetroot or slices of cucumber is an improvement.

KIPPERS.

Kippers are usually fried or grilled, but being tasty in themselves a good way of cooking them is to bake them in a Yorkshire tin half full of water in a moderate oven for 15—20 minutes.

BLOATERS.

These are best if soaked for 2—3 hours, boiled in water without salt or toasted on both sides before a clear fire.   Serve with pickled beetroot or hardboiled egg.

BLOATER PASTE.

METHOD.

Remove the fish from a boiled bloater, chop finely; add an equal quantity of grated cheese, season with pepper, cayenne and enough butter to make a soft paste.   Use for sandwiches or pack in little jars and cover tightly.

BLOATER SAVOURY.

METHOD.

Clean, soak as before and fillet.   Make a stuffing, using 1 dessertspoonful oatmeal, 1 teaspoonful dripping, chopped onion and seasoning for each bloater. Shape fish into rings, fill with stuffing, place in tin and bake 30 minutes.   Lift out and serve on rounds of toast.

FISH BALLER.

One pound of Fish (white, flaked).
One dessertspoonful of Cornflour.
One Egg.   One teaspoonful of Salt.
One gill of milk.

METHOD.

Skin, bone and flake fish or put through the mincer twice.   Pound in a wooden vessel with potato masher for 20 minutes till smooth and well mixed.   Have a little fat smoking hot in a clean frying pan and a plate of dry flour.   Take a spoonful of the mixture, dip it in the flour and form with the hand into flat cakes.   Fry a golden brown colour on both sides, about 5—7 minutes. Drain, and serve hot.

Note.—This quantity will make about 16 baller. The mixture may be beaten in a quart patent butter beater if obtainable.

PICKLED MACKEREL.

Three large Mackerel
One ounce of Pepper.
Three Nutmegs grated.
Mace or Mixed Herbs.
One handful of Salt.

METHOD.

Mix the seasonings together.   Wash, clean and dry mackerel, cut into 5 or 6 pieces.   Make two or three holes in each piece and fill these with seasoning, pushing it in with the finger; rub each piece all over with seasoning; fry in oil or dripping and set aside till cold.   Lay the pieces in a tight fitting vessel, cover with vinegar (will keep longer, if cold, boiled) cover tightly.   This will keep for some time and is very tasty.

SALT FISH PIE.

One pound of Salt Cod.
One pint of Bread Sauce.
One teaspoonful of chopped Parsley.
One tablespoonful of Butter.

METHOD.

Soak, boil, and flake fish.   Make the bread sauce, add the fish, butter and parsley; season with pepper and mustard.   Turn into pie-dish, brown in oven or cover with paste and bake 20-30 minutes.

UNCLE HENRY PIE.

One pound of Cod.
Two pounds of Potatoes.
One large Onion.
Pepper and Salt.

METHOD.

Wash, skin, bone the fish and cut into small pieces. Wash, pare, and slice potatoes. Skin and slice the onion thinly. Put these in a pan in layers having potatoes at top. Add two cups hot water and simmer gently for $\frac{1}{2}$ hour; turn out into piedish and serve hot.

SALT HERRING PIE.

Three Salt Herrings.
Half a pound of cold, mashed Potatoes.
One gill of Haricot Beans (cooked).
Small piece of Chopped Onion.
One tablespoonful of Vinegar.
Stock or Milk and Water.

METHOD.

Prepare herring in usual way, split, remove bones and fins and cut into pieces convenient for serving; dry, dust with flour. Place in a greased piedish, sprinkle over onion and pepper, put layer of beans, pour over milk and water; repeat until piedish is full. Mix the potatoes with milk or small piece of butter, spread over top, bake in a moderate oven for $\frac{3}{4}$-1 hour. A layer of apples is an improvement.

KEDGEREE.

One pound of cooked White Fish.
Half a pound of cooked Rice.
Four ounces of Margarine or Dripping.
Pepper and Salt and Nutmeg.
One teaspoonful of Curry Powder.
One hardboiled Egg (may be omitted).

METHOD.

Remove skin and bone, chop fish roughly, also white of egg. Melt butter, add all ingredients except yolk of egg; reheat thoroughly, pile on hot dish, decorate with yolk sieved on top.

FISH SALAD AND MAYONNAISE DRESSING.

Cold boiled Cod or Haddock, etc.
One Yolk of an Egg.
Salt, Pepper and Mustard.
Four tablespoonfuls of Salad Oil.
One to two tablespoonfuls of Malt Vinegar.

METHOD.

Flake fish, removing all skin and bones. Put yolk of egg and seasonings into basin, add salad oil drop by drop stirring all the time with a wooden spoon; when thick and smooth add vinegar gradually, amount depending on strength, until of the consistency of thick cream. Add fish to this; mix together, serve on a bed of lettuce and garnish with water cress, mustard cress or parsley.

Note.—Tinned salmon, cold boiled trout, may be

used in the same way and make a good mock salmon mayonnaise.

LOBSTER.

Lobster forms a nutritious food and moreover is seldom found diseased. The portions of the lobster which are not edible are the lungs, stomach and the intestinal vein. The coral or spawn found in the hen lobster during the breeding season is edible.

METHOD.

Wash well, tie the claws securely and throw the lobster (alive), head first, into a pan of boiling salted water. Boil gently for 20—30 minutes, according to size; avoid overcooking, which causes the flesh to become hard. When cold, break off claws and tail and divide the latter lengthwise by the line running from head to tail. Crack the claws with a hammer without injuring the flesh. Cold lobster meat is delicious served with mayonnaise.

CRAB.

The edible crab found in Shetland waters forms a delicious and nutritious dish if boiled (alive) for 10 minutes in boiling salted water. Most of the meat lies in the claws, but the dark soft kind, which is the liver, may also be eaten.

Meats.

PICKLED MUTTON.

Three and a half pounds of Salt.
Four quarts of Water.
Six ounces of Sugar.
Two to three ounces of Saltpetre.
About sixteen pounds of mutton.

METHOD.

Wipe meat and lay in salted water over night.
Pour off liquid. Bring salt and other ingredients to boil
in the water, allow to cool, pour into a stone crock, lay
in the meat and leave for 14—21 days; hang up and
use as required.

SALTING OF BEEF.

An average sized Shetland cow gives from 2-2¼
cwts. of beef, and 35-50 lb. of fat. Allow 10 lb. of
salt to 1 cwt. of beef or roughly 1 bushel to 1 cow.

METHOD.

Rub all the pieces of meat with salt and lay in a
tub over night; this draws out the extra blood which
might make the pickle impure. Next day, lift each

piece out, allow to drip, rub with salt and lay each piece out separately. Weigh the remainder of salt and weigh out an equal quantity of brown sugar. Pack the barrel with meat, putting a layer of salt and sugar between each until full; put on lid, which must have holes in it to allow of ventilation and set aside until salt becomes a brine. If this does not rise to the level of the top of the meat, make some extra pickle salt enough to float a potato, and pour this on.

Meat pickled in this way will keep 6—9 months. If pickle shows signs of decaying add fresh salt or turn out meat, wash, return to barrel with a little fresh salt strewn between each layer.

Note.—A specially strong tight barrel is required for salting. In many country districts it is possible to buy a " tiss " or barrel which has been brought from the south with beef.

PICKLED RUMP.

METHOD.

Make a pickle of salt and water strong enough to float a potato. Prepare the meat by rubbing well with salt as in " salting beef." Slit meat open to the centre; mix together a handful of salt and seasonings of pepper, cayenne, cinnamon and nutmeg; put this in centre of meat, fold together and tie around. Put meat in pickle and leave for 24 hours. Drain, hang outside in open air if possible for few hours or until dry; tie up firmly like a roll of bacon, and hang up until required. On account of the light salting, meat preserved in this way should be used before other cuts more heavily salted.

This cut was generally fried with onions or stewed.

SHETLAND SEASONING FOR SAUCERMEAT.

The poorer cuts of meat, generally beef, minced and seasoned with the following may be made into bronies and fried, or into meat loaf and baked.   A mixture of spices in the following proportion is first made.

Quarter of an ounce of Allspice.
Quarter of an ounce of Cloves.
Quarter of an ounce of Ginger.
Quarter of an ounce of White Pepper.
Quarter of an ounce of Black Pepper.
Eighth of an ounce of Mace.
Eighth of an ounce of Jamaica Pepper.
Eighth of an ounce of Cinnamon.

This along with 6 oz. salt, will season 12 lb. minced meat.

SAUCERMEAT BRONIES.

One pound of Saucermeat.
One pound of Minced Steak.
One teacupful of Breadcrumbs.
One tablespoonful of chopped Onion.
Pepper and Salt.
One Egg or Milk to moisten.

METHOD.

Mix all thoroughly together with the hand in a

basin; form into cakes about ¾ inch thick; fry on
both sides in smoking hot fat; reduce heat and allow to
cook through more slowly for 10—15 minutes; drain
and serve hot.

SPARLS.

When a cow was killed, certain parts were laid
aside for salting, drying and pickling.   The scraps of
meat, especially the fatty parts, also the gristle off
the breast and foreshoulder (best eaten when minced)
and all good scraps were used for " sparls."   If meat
was not very fat extra fat was added, generally " red-
dins."

METHOD.

Mince all or cut down finely; season with salt,
pepper, ginger, cinnamon and cloves—the amount of
spices depends largely on taste, but a goodly amount
of salt must be added.   When mixed a small piece was
tried out on the frying pan and if rather salty was considered right.

Take the large puddings, generally called the
sparls; wash well, rub dry, leave fat on; fill mixture
as in mealy puddings, pack very tightly.   When full
sew together or skewer with small wooden pins; lay in
tub, sprinkle with salt and leave over night.   In the
morning the salt will have melted into a brine.   Rub
sparls hard with coarse rag until clean—this removes
the " slime " and leaves puddings when dry clean and
white.   Rape up in the roof.   They are ready to eat

in three weeks to one month, but they will keep good for many months.

TO USE SPARLS:

Cut off amount required; peel off skin, cut in pieces and stew gently for 15—20 minutes, in a little water, which becomes a gravy.   If rather salt, blanch first in boiling water.

Note.—If liver is large, use a little more flour scarce, oatmeal was added to this gravy to make a thin porridge which could be supped without milk. Another method of cooking sparls was to cut them in thin slices and fry them.

PENSH PUDDINGS.

These are very similar to Sparls—only the poorer cuts of meat were used and more fat, so that they were not so rich in quality.

VIVDA.

This is mutton dried without salt in a skjo, which is a roughly built stone hut with slits to admit the wind for the purpose of drying fish and fresh mutton.

ROAST UDDER.

METHOD.

Cleanse thoroughly, parboil for half an hour;

spread with butter and roast in oven for one hour; stick with cloves, serve with gravy around.

TO STUFF :

Parboil, coat inside with yolk of egg, stuff with force meat and roast.

Udder may also be cut in neat pieces and stewed gently with onions in a little water.   Thicken later with a little flour to make a sauce.

STOVIES.

One and a half pounds of Mutton.
One pound of Potatoes.
Pepper and Salt.
One Onion.   Half a small Turnip.
One tablespoonful of Suet.

METHOD.

Cut mutton up finely; chop suet; put these into pan and pour on enough boiling water to cover; simmer gently for one hour.   Chop onion finely, grate turnip and potato; add these and stew gently for another hour; season and serve hot.

LIVER PUDDING.

One Sheep's Liver (medium-sized).
One and a half cupfuls of Suet.
One cup of Flour.
One Bag of Sheep, cleansed.

METHOD.

Soak bag in salt and water, scrape well and wash thoroughly.   Mash the liver in a basin with potato masher until soft, add chopped suet and flour and work all together until thoroughly mixed; season well with salt and pepper, fill bag with mixture about two-thirds full.   Sew together and boil for one hour.   Serve hot.

Note.—If liver is large, use a little more flour and suet in proportion.

SAVOURY SAUSAGES FROM LIGHTS,
OR
WHAT TO DO WITH LIGHTS.

METHOD.

Boil a calf's lights (any other may be used) in enough water to cover; chop finely; mash a small loaf down in the liquor in which lights were boiled; mix well.   Cut down 4 or 5 onions finely and fry lightly in fat (do not brown); add to lights; season well; add two beaten eggs and mix together.   Fill some cleaned sheep's intestines, close ends and fry as required.

LAMB'S KIDNEYS.

Six Kidneys.
Two tablespoonfuls of Fat.
One tablespoonful of Flour.
Half a pint of boiling water or Stock.

METHOD.

Soak for 20 minutes in cold water and salt; cut in

slices and sprinkle with salt and pepper; remove skin
and core; fry lightly in smoking hot fat; dredge with
flour; add boiling water; cook 5 minutes; season if
necessary and serve.   Kidneys must be cooked either
for a short time or for several hours — they become
tender after a few minutes' cooking, but soon toughen
and then need long slow cooking (about 2 hours) to
make them again tender.

Note.—Kidney added to a stew which lacks
flavour will improve it greatly, making a rich brown
sauce.

SHEEP'S BRAINS.

One Sheep's Brains.
Half a pint of Water and Milk or Stock.
One teaspoonful of Chopped Parsley.

METHOD.

Soak brains in salt and water for 2 hours; remove
skin; blanch; lay in cold water until cold (this stiffens
and whitens).   Simmer gently in liquid for 20 minutes;
add flour broken down; season and simmer for 10 minutes.   Dish on hot ashet.

TRIPE.

There are four kinds—Blanket, Monyplies or Book,
Black (most easily digested) and Honeycomb.   This is
a cheap food, easily digested when well cooked, but
must be thoroughly cleaned.

METHOD.

Wash in several waters until clean, soak in salt and water over night.   Blanch, *i.e.,* put on with cold water and bring to boil and pour away; put on again with plenty of cold water and salt, cover and cook slowly until tender, 7—8 hours.

CREAMED TRIPE.

Half a pint of Cooked Tripe.
Half a pint of White Sauce (see page 5).
One cooked Onion.   Pepper and Salt.

METHOD.

Make sauce, add tripe cut in neat sized pieces and onion chopped; reheat thoroughly for about 20 minutes; dish neatly.

BAKED TRIPE.

Half a pound of Cooked Tripe.
Two slices of buttered Bread.
One gill of Milk and Tripe Liquor.
One Egg.
Seasoning.

METHOD.

Cut tripe and bread into small pieces, put into piedish in layers.   Pour beaten egg and liquid over and bake for 30 minutes in moderate oven.

FRIED TRIPE IN BATTER.

METHOD.

Make a thick batter of flour and milk and seasoning—dip tripe cut into neat pieces, in the batter, fry in
fat until a golden brown.   Drain.

POTTED HEAD (I).

One Oxtail.
Two pounds of Hough.
One Knap Bone.

METHOD.

Wash and cover well with cold salted water and
simmer gently 5 to 6 hours until the bones are quite
loose and separate; remove these, chop meat in small
pieces, return to pan, season well, bring to boil in liquor
and when cool, turn into wet moulds.

POTTED HEAD (II).

One young Heifer's Head.
Four Feet with hoofs on.

METHOD.

HEAD :

Get the butcher to divide the head into four pieces;
lay in tub for a few hours with three handfuls of salt
and enough water to cover.   Wash well, drain, remove
eyes with sharp pointed knife or " sea-tullie."   If a

large pot is obtainable put all into pot, cover with water, add salt to taste and small bag of peppercorns. Bring to boil; skim; (if pot is too small boil cheek first, then other parts); boil for 2 to 3 hours until tender, dish and put stock away in crock to cool over night. In the morning the head stock will be found to have jellied. Remove fat; separate meat from bones and cut down in small pieces removing gristle, sinew and tough pieces, which can be boiled down later along with bones for second stock.

FEET:

Wash well, brushing between the hoofs; put in pan of boiling water (enough to cover hoofs); boil briskly 1½ hours; remove from pot; pour away water. When cool enough to handle remove hairy skin above hoof with sharp knife, also cut up between hoofs. Then with a screwdriver or strong knife, punch off hoof, dislocating it at the lower joint (the best way to do this is to cut from the back). The knuckle is held together by strong sinews. Cut foot in two. Put legs and feet into pot; cover with cold water; bring to boil; simmer 5 to 6 hours. Remove bones and put stock into crock. In the morning the feet stock will be found to have jellied. Remove fat (good for oatcakes and pastry). To make the meat shapes use equal parts of head stock and feet stock and about 1 lb. meat to 1 pint stock. Put meat and stock into pan, add seasonings of salt, pepper and grated nutmeg; bring to boil, boil for 10 minutes; allow to cool; dish in wet moulds and turn out when cold.

SHEEP'S HEAD BROTH.

One Sheep's Head.
Four quarts of Water.
One Turnip.   One Carrot.
Two Potatoes.   One small Onion.
Two sprigs of Parsley.
One teacupful of Barley.
Salt and Pepper.

METHOD.

Rub head with salt and soak over night in plenty of cold water to get rid of blood.   Put into a saucepan with the water; bring to boil; skim carefully.   Add vegetables cut into dice, simmer 1½ hours.   Serve head on hot dish and soup in tureen.

White sauce with chopped parsley added might be served with head.

DUNTER OR EIDER DUCK.

This is a species of seabird not often eaten because of its wild taste, but this is obviated by cooking in the following way :—

METHOD.

To save time and labour clip the feathers with sharp scissors close to the skin.   (These feathers make good pillows and the down off the breast and under the wings is invaluable for down quilts).   Cut off head and neck ; cut the skin down the back with sharp knife from head to tail and it will be found that the skin will

come off quite easily, taking with it all the fat which
lies under skin.   Remove meat from breast and legs—
the rest is of no use.   Have a frying pan of smoking
hot fat, brown the pieces of meat, put these into a stewpan with a little hot water, salt and peppercorns—stew
until tender, about 2 hours.   Dish in centre of hot
ashet with gravy, which is a rich brown, around.
Garnish with slices of lemon and small pieces of toast.

MALLARD DUCK.

These fly over from Norway and are shot in the
autumn.

METHOD.

Pluck and clean as a fowl. As this bird is usually
very fat it is best stuffed and roasted, or if not very
young, roast for 20—30 minutes, then stew until tender.
Use an ordinary chicken stuffing or a sweet stuffing
(currants and sugar instead of seasoning).

EBBCOCK.

This is a small species of bird found on the sea-
shore; a quantity of these are required to make a dish.

METHOD.

Pluck and clean in usual way.   Stew in pan with a
little water and seasoning until tender.   Fill a piedish
with these and cover with pastry, flaky or short crust;
bake 20—30 minutes in a fairly hot oven, until brown.
Serve hot or cold.

STARLING.

METHOD.

These are prepared and cooked similar to Ebbcock.

SNIPE.

METHOD.

Pluck and singe; make a slit round the right leg, remove the small bag and leave the rest; skewer with its own head by passing the beak through the legs; put a pat of butter on the breast, lay on toast, roast for 7 to 10 minutes and serve on toast.

They may also be cooked in a pie or stewed.

WOODCOCK.

METHOD.

Prepare as for Snipe; bake 20 to 30 minutes. Serve with chipped potatoes and brown breadcrumbs heated and served in sauceboat with pat of butter on top.

They may also be stuffed with potato (one-third) and breadcrumb (two-third) stuffing seasoned with sage.

IRISH STEW.

One pound of Mutton.
One dozen of Potatoes.
Two Onions.
Salt and Pepper.   Water.

METHOD.

Wipe meat; cut into neat pieces; slice onion; peel two potatoes and slice thinly. Put meat, potato and onion into stewpan, add ½ pint boiling water and simmer gently 1 hour. Peel rest of potatoes, cut in halves or thick slices; add to stew; season well; cook for ½ hour longer or till potatoes are tender. Serve meat in centre of ashet and potatoes around.

BROWN STEW.

One pound of Stewing Steak
Two ounces of Dripping.
Two Onions.
One ounce of Flour.
One Turnip.   One Carrot.
Salt and Pepper.
Water.

METHOD.

Wipe meat; cut into neat pieces; chop onion. Make dripping smoking hot in an iron stewpan or frying pan. Fry meat and lift on to plate; fry onion lightly, then flour until brown. Add 1 pint of hot water gradually, stir until it boils. Return meat to pan and simmer gently. Prepare carrot and turnip; cut in neat pieces; add, cook slowly for 1½ to 2 hours, stirring frequently. Serve meat in centre of ashet with vegetables around.

SAVOURY BALLS.

(Excellent to serve with Brown Stew).

>Six ounces of Flour.
>Three ounces of Suet.
>Two teaspoonfuls of chopped Onion.
>Two teaspoonfuls of chopped Parsley.
>Half a teaspoonful of Baking Powder.
>Half a teaspoonful of Salt.
>Cold Water.

METHOD.

Chop suet finely and mix with other ingredients; add enough water to make a firm paste; divide into little balls, roll in flour and drop into stew $\frac{1}{2}$ hour before serving.

SEA PIE.

This is similar to Brown Stew.   Omit onion and parsley from Savoury Ball mixture; roll out into round, size of stewpan; place crust on top of meat at half-time; when done cut neatly in four and serve on top of stew.

STEWED RABBIT.

>One Rabbit.   Three Onions.
>Two tablespoonfuls of Fat.
>Three tablespoonfuls of Flour.
>One pint of Water.
>Pepper and Salt.

METHOD.

Skin, wash and joint the rabbit.   Dip in seasoned flour and fry a golden brown on both sides.   Cut the onions in slices and fry also.   Remove from pan, add remainder of flour, mix with dripping, add hot water or stock; bring to boil and season.   Return meat and onions to pan and simmer gently for 1½—2 hours. Dish neatly and pour gravy around.

REISTED GOOSE.

When not convenient to use a whole goose at a time, it was often cut in pieces, laid in salt for 3—4 days, then dried and hung up to reist in smoke.

MINCE.

QUICK METHOD.

Half a pound of Steak, minced.
Half a pound of Saucermeat.
Two cupfuls of Water.
Two tablespoonfuls of Flour.

METHOD.

Mix steak and saucermeat in pan, pour over boiling water, stew gently for 20 minutes; break down flour with water, add with more seasoning if required, cook for 10 minutes.   Serve hot with small pieces of toast. The addition of an onion chopped finely is an improvement.

CORNED BEEF HASH.

One small tin of Corned Beef.
Six medium-sized Onions.
Two tablespoonfuls of Flour.
Salt, Pepper, small pinch of Curry Powder.

METHOD.

Peel and slice onions into saucepan.   Put in three
cups of cold water.   Bring to boil and simmer until
onions are tender.   Break down flour with a little cold
water.   Add to contents of pan and stir until thick and
cooked.   Cut up corned beef into cubes, put into pan
and allow to heat through; add seasonings and serve
hot.

Quickly made and a splendid emergency dish for
the country either as breakfast, dinner or supper with
toast, potatoes or bread.

Meal Dishes.

MEALY PUDDINGS.

METHOD.

After the pudding skins have been emptied, soak in salt and water overnight; cut into lengths about 18 inches and holding them under a running tap, let water run through until it runs out clear. Be very careful not to allow anything from the inside to get on to the fat on outside of skin. Leave in basin of cold water. Mix filling as follows:—For 6 lengths of skin allow about—

> Four cupfuls of fine Oatmeal.
> Two ounces of Flour.
> Six ounces of Suet (more or less according to amount of fat on skins).
> One Onion finely chopped.
> One teaspoonful of Salt.
> Half a teaspoonful of Pepper.

METHOD.

Chop suet and onion, mix all together, moisten with about half a cup of hot water.

Filling the Skins : The aim in this is to fill the skins by reversing so that the inner side does on no account touch the outside with the fat on. Hold one skin over a plate, turn the top inwards about one inch, hold tightly perpendicularly in left hand over mouth of basin and fill with right hand, packing closely. The filled skin will slip down, so that the whole skin will turn outside in without the fatty side coming in contact with the other side which has not yet been thoroughly cleansed. Sew both ends to prevent the mixture coming out. Wash well, scrub gently if necessary.

Cooking : Plunge into boiling salted water and boil steadily for $\frac{3}{4}$—1 hour according to thickness of skins. When cooked remove from pan and keep in cool place and when required may be reheated in boiling water or cut in slices and fried.

Note.—The water in which the puddings are boiled must be immediately thrown away, and the pot well washed.

SWEET PUDDINGS.

Instead of onions and seasonings as in mealy puddings, sugar and currants may be substituted to advantage.

> One cupful of Flour.
> One dessertspoonful of Sugar.
> One tablespoonful of Currants.
> Pinch of Baking Soda.
> Pinch of Cream of Tartar.
> Water.

METHOD.

Mix to a dropping consistency so that mixture may be put in with a spoon.

Note.—Puddings made with one part oatmeal and three parts flour are freer. An average flour pudding requires equal suet to flour; if there is excess of fat on the skins, use less suet; if fat runs short use a little more water in mixing.

BURSTIN PUDDINGS.

These were generally made with pigs' puddings, as the lard in the puddings amalgamated better with the burstin.

HOONSKA (BLACK PUDDINGS).

Flour.   Minced Suet.
Salt and Pepper.   Blood.

METHOD.

Procure a pail of blood from a healthy animal, preferably a cow. As it quickly congeals on cooling, it will probably be in a solid mass; if there is any fluid around it pour this away. Rub as much blood as you think you will require through a sieve with a wooden spoon. In the old days this was done by taking a clean wisp of straw and pressing the blood through it. To each cup of blood add one cup of warm water, (not boiling) and beat these together to thoroughly mix and remove all clots until quite smooth. The blood must not be too strong or puddings will be very black and hard. Mix together flour, minced suet and seasonings as in Mealy Puddings, add enough blood and

water to make a thin dropping mixture of the consistency of porridge.   Cut the skins in short lengths,
prepare and fill as in Mealy Puddings.   This mixture
being thinner may be poured from a jug with a good
spout or filled in with a spoon.   Sew the ends or close
with a thin wooden pin (both ends may be pinned together forming a circle).   Finally wash the puddings
again; see that the mixture is equally divided throughout the skins. Plunge into boiling salted water and boil
for a few minutes.   With a darning needle pierce the
skins to let out the air; boil slowly for ½ hour.   Remove from water and hang up to dry.   When required
reheat in a pan of boiling water or slice neatly and fry.
The addition of minced onion is considered by some an
improvement and may be added according to taste.

TAR-TIN-PURRIE.

In olden times kail and potatoes was a favourite
supper dish, or kail alone.   As the vegetables were
cleaned, the liquid in which it was boiled was kept overnight and used to make the morning porridge with; it
was made rather thin and could be supped without milk
if this were scarce.   An improvement on this would be
the addition of a piece of mutton or ham to the liquid
when cooking.

KAIL AND KNOCKED CORN.

METHOD.

Into a pot of boiling water put some kail, small
piece of pork or reisted mutton and some corn.   Boil

all thoroughly together and serve together hot with seasonings.

VIRPA (SOWANS).

In the old days, when grinding corn it was usual to put sids (outer husk) aside for Virpa.   This was put into a kirn or wooden "span" and covered with water; this was allowed to stand 8—10 days, strained, and the juice boiled and supped.   The following is a modern method of Virpa.

> One pound of fine Oatmeal.
> Three pounds of Wheaten Meal.
> Two gallons of Water.

METHOD.

Put meal into a stone crock, stir in water (luke-warm) and let it stand 5—8 days till sour (depends on heat).   Pour off clear liquid, let this stand a few days till rather sharp; this is the swats and makes a refreshing drink.   The remainder in the crock will resemble a thick starch; add 2 pints cold water which will make it of the consistency of cream.   Strain through a cheese cloth over a colander.   The liquid which passes through contains practically all the nutritious properties of the oatmeal and only the outer husk is left.   Gentle rubbing with a wooden spoon and finally squeezing the cloth with the hand will hasten the process.   Thus as will be readily understood, we have the strength of the oatmeal in the easiest digested form; therefore this dish is especially good for invalids or people of impaired digestions.

To Cook Virpa: Measure the required quantity into a pan, allowing 1 gill per person—add 2 gills water (hot) per person, 1 teaspoonful salt and bring to boil stirring continually, otherwise it will stick to the bottom. Boil gently for 10 minutes till thick and clear looking; dish and sup with milk or cream.

PORRIDGE.

Half a pint of Water.
One ounce of Oatmeal.
Pinch of Salt.

METHOD.

Have the water boiling, add salt; sprinkle in the oatmeal very gradually, stirring well until all is added and brought to boil. Boil gently for 20 minutes for fine oatmeal and half an hour for coarse oatmeal.

MILGRUEL.

This is the same as porridge, except that milk is used instead of water.

BEREMEAL PORRIDGE.

Substitute beremeal for oatmeal and use method given in Porridge.

SKIRLEY IN THE POT.

Two breakfastcupfuls of Oatmeal.
Two Onions.
One tablespoonful of Fat.
Little Water.

METHOD.

Into a pan put water, fat and onions (sliced) and bring to boil; add pepper and salt. Stir meal quickly in until it absorbs the liquid, the mixture should be rather dry. Cook it quickly for a few minutes, but do not let it boil. Serve hot with potatoes.

OATMEAL BROTH.

Quarter of a pound of Reisted Mutton.
Two quarts of Water.
Quarter of a pound of Oatmeal (4 handfuls).
Three or four medium Potatoes.
Pepper.

METHOD.

Cut mutton into small pieces, put into pan with water, bring to boil and boil for 20 minutes; add oatmeal as in porridge, boil 10 minutes; add potatoes pared and sliced thinly, cook another 10 minutes. Season to taste. The consistency should be thin; if allowed to boil in and become thick and porridgy, add more water.

LEYVERIN.

METHOD.

Take the liquid that a ham has been boiled in and while boiling thicken it with flour or meal, broken down to a paste. Boiling milk or water may be used instead of ham liquid.

STOORADRINK.

METHOD.

Heat some swats in a pan and into it stir a few handfuls of oatmeal, mix together.

PRAMM, OR BURSTIN AND MILK.

METHOD.

Put the burstin in a basin; heat some milk and pour over, serve hot. This may also be made with fine oatmeal. Some people prefer cold milk poured on burstin, and some " kirnmilk " instead of milk.

BROSE.

METHOD.

Into a basin put some cold oatmeal, pepper and salt; add boiling water, stirring well. Serve with butter or milk.

Sometimes the " broe " from kail or turnips was used or a good meat stock.

WIRTIGLUGS.

METHOD.

Wirt is a sweet infusion of malt.   Into a basin put some meal and pour the hot wirt over to make the consistency of brose.

GLUGS.

METHOD.

Put equal parts of oatmeal and burstin into a basin, mix with water into a " bronie."   This was eaten uncooked.

FATTY BRONIES.

Half a pound of fine Oatmeal.
Quarter of a teaspoonful of Salt.
One to two tablespoonfuls of Dripping or
    Butter.

METHOD.

Mix together oatmeal and salt; pour a little hot water over the fat; add this and enough water to make a cake stiff enough to stand on end; brown in front of fire.

YULE BRONIES.

These were cakes made of rye meal and fat, with the edges nipped out to represent the sun's rays.

v

BLANDA MEAL.

This was obtained by mixing bere and oats and sowing them together.

BLANDA BREAD.

This is a bannock prepared in the usual way, using oatmeal and beremeal mixed.

TIVLACH.

This is a thick cake of coarse meal.

SNODDIE.

A thick cake or bannock baked among the ashes.

SKORPER.

This is a round cake of bread, resembling what is known in Scotland as a cookie.

SEABIDDIES.

The name given to large bannocks which fishermen take with them to the haaf.

Puddings, etc.

PLAIN SUET PUDDING.

Half a pound of Flour.
Four ounces of Suet.
One teaspoonful of Baking Powder.
One gill of Water or Milk.

METHOD.

Mix the dry ingredients; shred and chop the suet finely, mix together, add milk to make a soft dropping consistency; turn into a greased basin, cover with greased paper and steam for 1—1½ hours.

Note.—The addition of 2 oz. of sugar, with sultanas, currants, figs, cocoanut or spice make a richer pudding.

BAKED SUET ROLL.

Use same ingredients as in Plain Suet Pudding. Mix to a soft dough, roll out on board, spread with jam, wet the edges, roll up and bake in a moderate oven for 20—30 minutes or boil in a floured cloth for 2 hours.

SUET DUMPLINGS.

Half a pint of Milk.
One pound of Flour.
Half a pound of Suet.
Two Eggs.
Half a pound of Currants.
Three teaspoonfuls of Ginger.
Two teaspoonfuls of Salt.

METHOD.

Mix as in Plain Suet Pudding to make a light paste; form into dumplings the size of a large egg, dip in flour; have a pan of *boiling* water, drop in gently, boil half an hour.

Note.—This may also be boiled in a cloth or steamed in a basin.

PLAIN PLUM PUDDING.

Four ounces of Breadcrumbs.
Two ounces of Flour.
Three ounces of Suet.
Two ounces of Raisins.
Two ounces of Sultanas.
Two ounces of Currants.
Pinches of Cinnamon, Ginger, Allspice, Nutmeg, Cloves, Salt.
One teaspoonful of Baking Powder.
Two Eggs.   Half a gill of Milk.
Two ounces of Sugar.   One ounce of Peel.

METHOD.

Clean the fruit and stone the raisins; chop the

peel, shred and chop the suet finely.   Mix all the dry ingredients in a basin, beat up the eggs and add with milk, mix thoroughly—mixture should not be too stiff; turn into buttered basin (¾ full) cover with greased paper and steam 5—6 hours.   The pudding may also be boiled in a cloth (3 hours) or put in a basin (full) covered with a floured cloth and boiled.

PLUM PUDDING.

Half a pound of Breadcrumbs.
Two ounces of Flour.
Half a pound of Suet.
Half a pound of Valencias.
Half a pound of Sultanas.
Half a pound of Currants.
Two ounces of mixed Peel.
Two ounces of Citron Peel.
Two ounces of Almonds.
One teaspoonful of mixed Spice.
One Lemon.   Four Eggs.
Half a pound of Demerara Sugar.
Pinch of Salt.   Milk.

METHOD.

Prepare as in Plain Plum Pudding, adding enough milk to make a moist consistency.   Steam for 8 hours or boil for 5 hours; when reheating boil for 2 hours at least.

Note.—Figs, dates, apples or nuts may be substituted.

CHEAP RICE PUDDING.

Quarter of a pound of Rice.
Half a pound of Raisins.

METHOD.

Mix together rice and raisins, tie in a floured cloth giving rice room to swell; plunge into pan of boiling water, boil for 2 hours; turn out, pour over melted butter, sprinkle with sugar and nutmeg.

COCOANUT RICE PUDDING.

Quarter of a pound of Rice.
Two ounces of Sugar.
Two ounces of Cocoanut.
One pint of Milk and one pint of Water,
or
One quart of Milk.

METHOD.

Wash the rice, put all ingredients into greased piedish, stir to dissolve sugar; bake in a slow oven at least 2 hours.

FRUIT SALAD.

Two Bananas.
Two Oranges.   Two Apples.
One small tin of Pineapple.
One cup of stewed Prunes.

METHOD.

Turn the pineapple into a basin, cut into small pieces, and oranges, bananas and apples peeled and cut into neat pieces; add prunes; mix together, sprinkle with sugar and leave for a few hours.

Note.—Any other fruit in season may be used.

SAGO MOULD (WITHOUT MILK.)

Four ounces of Sago or Tapioca.
One and a quarter pints of Water.
Two tablespoonfuls of Syrup.
      or two tablespoonfuls of Jam—preferably
      Black Currant Jelly).
Rind and Juice of one Lemon.

METHOD.

Place water and lemon rind in pan and bring to boil; remove lemon rind, add sago and stir until it boils, boil for 10 minutes; add syrup and lemon juice and boil for another 10 minutes or until sago is quite clear.   Pour into wet mould and when cold turn out.

CARAMEL TAPIOCA.

Quarter of a pound of Tapioca.
Quarter of a pound of Brown Sugar.
One pint of Water.
Flavouring.

METHOD.

Soak tapioca overnight and boil as usual, allowing about 1 pint water to $\frac{1}{4}$ lb. tapioca; the mixture should

be rather thick.   Add sugar and stir until it has melted
into a syrup; dish and allow to get quite cold.

Bread, Scones, Cakes, etc.

SCONES.

In a large household where these are made daily, it is a good plan to mix flour ready for baking in a large quantity—but unless kept in a tin in a thoroughly dry place, the raising agent loses its power.

Ten pounds of Flour.
Four ounces of Cream of Tartar.
Two ounces of Baking Soda.
Small handful of Salt.

METHOD.

Mix well together, pass through a sieve, store and use as required with run sweet milk or buttermilk that is not very sour.

Substitute for Buttermilk.—In town and in the winter time buttermilk is very often difficult to obtain, but a good substitute is always at hand. When pouring potatoes put a jug of this potato water aside, allow to stand for a few days until it sours; use instead of buttermilk.

FLOUR BANNOCKS.

One pound of Flour.
One teaspoonful (large) Baking Soda.
One teaspoonful of Cream of Tartar.
One teaspoonful of Salt.
Buttermilk or Sour Milk.

METHOD.

Mix the dry ingredients together, make into a soft dough with the buttermilk, just as soft as can be easily handled. Turn on to a floured board, turn in the rough edges and roll out gently until $\frac{1}{4}$—$\frac{1}{2}$ inch thick. Cut in squares or rounds, bake on a moderately hot girdle or in fairly hot oven for 10—15 minutes. Roll out slightly thinner for the girdle; if sweet milk or milk and water is used, add double the amount of cream of tartar.

BEREMEAL BANNOCKS.

One pound of Flour.
Half a pound of Beremeal.
One teaspoonful of Salt.
Two small teaspoonfuls of Cream of Tartar.
Two small teaspoonfuls of Baking Soda.
Sweet Milk and Water.
   (*If Buttermilk is used, One teaspoonful of Cream of Tartar.*)

METHOD.

Prepare and bake as Flour Scones either in oven or on girdle.

Note.—More baking soda is required to counteract the acids found in beremeal; the scones when baked should have a pinkish tinge.

BRIDE'S BONN.

Four ounces of Flour.
Two to Three ounces of Butter.
One ounce of Sugar.
One teaspoonful of Carraway Seeds.
Milk to mix.

METHOD.

Rub butter into flour, add other ingredients. Mix to a fairly stiff dough; bake over gridiron or in a fairly hot oven for 10—12 minutes.

PLOY SCONE.

This is similar to Bride's Bonn, except that sugar is omitted. This was eaten at 12 o'clock tea by the ladies.

TATTIE BANNOCKS.

Half a pound of cold Potatoes.
About two ounces of Flour.
About half a gill of milk.
Pinch of Salt.

METHOD.

Mash the potatoes and add the salt; knead as much flour into this as it will take up, and add enough milk to make a stiff dough.   Roll out very thinly on a floured board; cut into rounds, and prick with a fork. Bake on a hot girdle for about 5 minutes, turning when half cooked.   Serve very hot.   These may also be baked on the hearth.

TATTIE PANCAKES.

Six Potatoes (medium).
One Egg.
One tablespoonful of Sugar.
Milk.

METHOD.

Pare potatoes, grate into pot of cold water; allow to stand for a few hours, then gently pour off water. This takes away any bitterness and softens the starch. Take the residue and mix with egg, sugar and milk to a batter.   Cook as in dropped scones.

OATCAKES.

One teacupful of fine Oatmeal.
One teaspoonful of melted Fat (bacon fat or dripping).
Pinch of Salt.
Pinch of Baking Soda.

METHOD.

Mix dry ingredients together, measure fat into a cup and add hot water, mix to a stiff dough and quickly knead into round and roll out thinly; cut into four and bake on a hot girdle, until edges begin to curl up--or cakes may be rolled thickly and baked on both sides; crisp off in a moderate oven.

Note.—Do not mix a large quantity at a time as when mixture gets cold it breaks and is difficult to roll out.

ROCK BUNS.

Half a pound of Flour.
Four ounces of Sugar.
Four ounces of Currants.
Three ounces of Butter.
One ounce of Peel.
One teaspoonful of Baking Powder.
Pinch of Ginger or Spice.
One Egg.   Milk.

METHOD.

Sieve flour, rub in butter, add other dry ingredients —currants cleaned, peel shredded.   Beat egg, add a little milk and mix to stiff consistency; place in little heaps on a greased baking tray and bake in a hot oven for 15 minutes.   A softer consistency is required if baked in patty tins.

BUTTER BISCUITS.

Half a pound of Flour.
Four ounces of Butter or Margarine.
Cold Water.
Yolk of Egg (if wished).

METHOD.

Sieve flour and pinch of salt into basin, rub in butter; mix this to a stiff dough with water, turn on to floured board, roll thinly, prick well, cut into rounds or squares; place on greased tin and bake in a moderate oven for 10—15 minutes.

CHEESE BISCUITS.

Use the recipe for Butter Biscuits with the addition of 2 oz. grated cheese and yolk of egg to bind; bake in a rather quick oven for 10 minutes.

SHORTBREAD.

Four onuces of Flour.
Two ounces of Rice Flour.
Four ounces of Butter.
Two ounces of Castor Sugar.

METHOD.

Sieve flour, rice flour and sugar into basin; add butter and work together with hand until a smooth dough is obtained; either place in floured short bread mould or roll out and cut into biscuits, prick all over, place in greased and papered tin; bake in steady oven till beginning to brown—if a thick cake moderate the heat and crisp off slowly for about an hour.

ECONOMICAL SHORTBREAD.

Fourteen ounces of Flour.
Two ounces of Rice Flour.
Eight ounces of Margarine or Butter.
Four ounces of Sugar.

METHOD.

Mix as in Shortbread, cook in a rather slow oven till browned and crisp.

ROLLED OATS SHORTBREAD.

Four ounces of Flour.
Four ounces of Rolled Oats.
Four ounces of Butter.
Two ounces of Brown Sugar.

METHOD.

Cream butter and sugar together and work in flour and oats to a paste; roll out, cut into rounds and bake in a moderate oven 10—15 minutes.

CURRANT LOAF.

Four pounds of Baker's Dough.
Two pounds of Raisins.
Two pounds of Currants.
One pound of Sugar.
One pound of Butter.
Quarter of a pound of Blanched Almonds.
Quarter of a pound of Candied Peel.
One ounce of Ginger.
One ounce of Cinnamon.
Half an ounce of Jamaica Pepper.
One Nutmeg grated.

METHOD.

Mix butter with the dough, working it in with the hands. Take off one pound of the dough, and roll it out with a little flour, and cut off as much as will form the top crust of the bun. With the other part of the pound line a greased baking tin. Have the fruit ready cleaned and the almonds blanched and chopped, also the peel minced finely.   Add the spices and sugar to the fruit, etc., and mix all with the remaining dough (there should be three pounds dough left).   Mix all well together in a large basin, and then put it into the lined tin.   Wet the top edge of the dough, place on the top crust, and prick over the surface with a fork.   Bake in a steady oven for three or four hours, but do not let it burn.   When the top is browned, brush it over with beaten egg to glaze it.

CURRANT CAKE.

Half a pound of Flour.
Three ounces of Butter.
Four ounces of Castor Sugar.
Four ounces of Currants.
Two Eggs.
One teaspoonful of Baking Powder.
Half a gill of Milk.

METHOD.

Sieve flour, rub in butter; clean currants, shred peel and mix all dry ingredients.   Beat eggs and milk and mix together to a soft dropping consistency.   Turn into prepared tin and bake for 1½ hours in steady oven.

Note.—Sultanas or cocoanut (3 oz.) or 1 dessertspoonful carraway seeds may be used instead of currants, each giving their own name to cake.

BACHELOR CAKE (WITHOUT EGGS).

One pound of Flour.
Half a pound of Sugar.
Quarter of a pound of Butter.
Four ounces of Currants or Sultanas.
Two teaspoonfuls of Baking Soda.
Half an ounce of Ginger.
Half an ounce of Cinnamon.
Pinch of Spice.
Buttermilk.

METHOD.

Mix dry ingredients, rub in butter and mix with buttermilk to a rather soft consistency; turn into tin, well greased, and bake in moderate oven 1—1½ hours. Test with warm knitting needle in centre which should come out clean.

CHRISTMAS CAKE.

Three quarters of a pound of Flour.
Half a pound of Butter.
Half a pound of Sugar.
Half a pound of Currants.
Quarter of a pound of Sultanas.
Four Eggs.
Two ounces of Peel.
Two ounces of Cherries.
Two ounces of Walnuts.
Two ounces of Ginger.
Two ounces of Almonds.
  Icing—Two pounds of Icing Sugar; Three Eggs; Half a pound of Ground Almonds.

METHOD.

Cream butter and sugar and beat in eggs one by one with a little flour; add the cleaned fruit, peel, walnuts, etc., chopped roughly, and rest of flour—mixture should not be too soft.   Turn into tin well greased and lined with greased paper, bake in a steady oven, only moderately hot, for 3—4 hours.

Icing.—Mix ground almonds and ½ lb. sugar well together, bind with yolk of egg and flavouring to a paste, roll out into a round; brush top of cake with egg and lay almond paste on, put into cool oven to firm 15—20 minutes.   Sieve the rest of the icing sugar, add whites of egg gradually, mix to a soft paste and spread on cake, make smooth with knife dipped in hot water; decorate and set aside to harden.

AMERICAN TEA CAKE.

Two cupfuls of Flour.
Half a teaspoonful of Baking Soda.
One teaspoonful of Cream of Tartar.
Two tablespoonfuls of Margarine.
Half a cupful of Sugar.
One or two Eggs.
Cinnamon.
Breadcrumbs.

METHOD.

Mix dry ingredients, except sugar; rub in the margarine; add the sugar.   Beat the egg (if one egg add a little milk).   Mix all together till the mixture drops from the spoon, turn into a flat greased cake tin;

do not scrape your bowl.   Into the bowl put enough
sugar, breadcrumbs and cinnamon to form a crumbly
mixture with the leavings.   Work it into crumbs with
the fingers; press this all over top of cake, bake in a
hot oven till done.

GINGERBREAD.

Half a pound of Flour.
Two ounces of Butter.
Two ounces of Sugar.
Two ounces of Treacle.
Half a teaspoonful of Baking Soda.
Half a teaspoonful of Ground Ginger.
Half a teaspoonful of Mixed Spice.
Quarter of a teaspoonful of Salt.
Buttermilk.

METHOD.

Grease and flour a cake tin.   Melt together butter
and treacle; mix together dry ingredients, and add to
them the butter and treacle and enough buttermilk to
make a soft mixture.   Bake in a moderate oven till
firm in centre, about $\frac{3}{4}$ hour.

YEAST BUNS.

Half a pound of Flour.
One ounce of Yeast.
One teaspoonful of Castor Sugar.
Three Gills of Milk.

METHOD.

Sieve flour, cream yeast and sugar and add luke-warm milk; add to centre of flour gradually stirring to make a smooth batter.   Cover with cloth and set in warm place for 1 hour to rise.

Prepare in basin :—

One and a quarter pounds of Flour.
Quarter of a pound of Butter.
Quarter of a pound of Sultanas.
Two ounces of Candied Peel.
Quarter of a pound of Castor Sugar.
Two Eggs.

Rub butter into flour, add other dry ingredients; when sponge in first basin has risen, beat in dry ingredients from the second basin with the beaten eggs.   Mix very well, beating for about 5 minutes.   Cover and set to rise again for 1½ hours.   Form into small buns, place on greased and floured tray, prove for 10—15 minutes in warm place; bake in hot oven 15—20 minutes. When ready, brush with sugar and milk to glaze.

VIENNA BREAD.

One pound of Flour.
One teaspoonful of Salt.
One ounce of Butter.
One teaspoonful of Castor Sugar.
Half an ounce of Yeast.
Half a pint of Milk.   One Egg.

METHOD.

Sieve flour and salt into basin, rub in butter. Cream yeast and sugar until liquid (mix together with teaspoon). Add the tepid milk and egg to the middle of the flour; mix together to a smooth dough, cover with a cloth and set in a warm place to rise 1—2 hours. Remove from basin on to floured board and with the hand form into fancy shapes; place on greased baking sheet and set to prove in warm place for 15 minutes. Bake in quick oven 20—30 minutes; brush over with melted butter while hot.

OATMEAL MACAROONS.

Half a pound of Flour.
One and a quarter cupfuls of Rolled Oats.
Half a cupful of Brown Sugar.
Quarter of a pound of Butter.
One teaspoonful of Baking Powder.
Half a cupful of Cocoanut.
One Egg.

METHOD.

Rub the butter into flour, add other dry ingredients. Beat egg, add with enough milk to make a rather stiff dough; roll out to ¼ inch thickness, cut into rounds and bake on a greased tin in a fairly hot oven 10—15 minutes. They may also be baked in little rough heaps like Rock Cakes.

USTEEN.

METHOD.

Heat some buttermilk with sweet milk until the curd separates from the whey; drain this away and press the curd in a cheesecloth. In short, this is a method of making junket without rennet. Run milk may also be used.

Sometimes sherry or any acid comforting liquid which will reduce milk to curd and whey was added. The curd was eaten first, then the whey drunk afterwards.

STRUBBA.

This is milk which is just on turning point (run) but not lappered in thick clots.

METHOD.

Whip up till of the consistency of cream.

HUNGMILL.

METHOD.

Save any portions of cream that may have gone sour; put into a small flannel bag and drain all the whey away.

KLABBA.

This is junket set thick by the action of yearnin or butterwort.

BEEST.

This is the first milk from a cow after calving. If the very first is used this is very strong and should have a little water added.

METHOD.

To the milk add salt; put into pan and stir gently only until it begins to set, then allow to slowly set into a cheese. If made in a three legged pot, when half done put a little fire on lid; this makes a firmer cheese on top.

KLOKS, OR BEEST PUDDING.

METHOD.

Put beest into piedish with sugar to sweeten, bake in moderate oven until set, 20—30 minutes. Salt, cinnamon or carraway seeds may also be added according to taste.

Invalid Dishes.

The food used should be the best of its kind, fresh, nourishing, appetising and easily digested. Serve little and often; prepare daintily with special regard to cleanliness. Season sparingly.

BEEF TEA.

This is not a food but a stimulating drink.
> Half a pound of lean Beef.
> Half a pint of Water.
> Pinch of Salt.

METHOD.

Shred beef finely, remove fat; put into a jar with cold water and salt; stand for $\frac{1}{2}$ hour, cover closely. Stand jar in pan of cold water; bring this slowly to boil and simmer gently for 3—4 hours; stir contents of jar and strain into cup. Remove any traces of grease with paper; season and serve with toast.

BARLEY WATER.

> One and a half ounces of Barley.
> One pint of cold Water.
> Three strips of Lemon Rind.
> One teaspoonful of Sugar.
> Pinch of Salt.

METHOD.

Wash and scald the barley, put into saucepan with water, lemon rind, sugar and salt. Simmer gently 1½— 2 hours, strain.

PIRR, OR BROCHIN.

Excellent cure for a chill if taken piping hot at night immediately before retiring; it is also a refreshing drink.

Two tablespoonfuls of Oatmeal.
Little Milk.
Half a teaspoonful of Cream of Tartar.
One teaspoonful of Sugar.

METHOD.

Mix ingredients in a warm jug, break down with milk to a smooth paste; add about half a pint boiling water, serve hot.

MUTTON BROTH.

Half a pound of Lean Mutton.
One pint of Water.
One ounce of Barley.
One small Carrot.
One small Turnip.
Seasoning.

METHOD.

Cut meat into inch pieces, removing fat; wash and scald barley; put both into pan with cold water, bring slowly to boil and simmer gently for 1 hour.   Add carrot and turnip, simmer gently for 1 hour longer; remove mutton and vegetables, season.   If desired, broth may be strained.

STEAMED FISH.

METHOD.

Fillet a whiting or haddock, roll up fillets from head to tail; place on a greased plate, cover with a buttered paper, place above pan of boiling water, steam for 10—15 minutes.

Note.—White fish is suitable for invalids because the fat, which is not so easily digested as the flesh of the fish, is contained in the liver.

PECTORAL DRINK.

(Frequently used during measles.)
One gallon of Water.
Half a pound of Barley.
Quarter of a pound of Split Figs.
Half an ounce of Liquorice.
Quarter of a pound of Stoned Raisins.

METHOD.

Boil all together until reduced to half, strain and use.

SWEETBREADS.

These are found in the lamb or calf and must be used when fresh, as they spoil very quickly.

METHOD.

Soak in cold water for 1 hour.　Drain, plunge into boiling salted water and cook slowly for 20 minutes.　Drain, plunge into cold water to keep them white and firm.　Remove any membrane.　Sweetbreads should be parboiled in this manner for subsequent cooking; then they may be broiled, creamed, baked, braised, etc.

Miscellaneous.

BLAAND.

This is a refreshing drink made by pouring enough hot water on buttermilk to make it separate; the curd is drained, pressed and served as Kirnmilk. The whey is allowed to stand until it reaches the fermenting, sparkling stage.

EGGALOORIE.

This is caudle, offered to women visiting a mother on the birth of a child.

METHOD.

Into a pan put $\frac{1}{2}$ pint milk, and pinch of salt; bring to boil and pour this over 2 beaten eggs; return to pan, bring slowly almost to boiling point and serve.

WHIPKULL.

One dozen Yolks of Eggs (fresh).
One pound of Castor Sugar.
One pint of Rum or Mead.
One quart of sweet Cream.

METHOD.

Beat the yolks and sugar together till thick and creamy, add cream and rum or any spirit. Allow to stand for some time until ingredients are thoroughly blended; pour into glasses and serve.

STOOINS.

This is the tops of young cabbage leaves cut off and boiled as greens.

SEAWEED.

In Shetland seaweed was seldom used, unless in cases of extremity; but a family in poverty was known to exist for a short time on honeywirt, the heads of which are eaten raw.

MACARONI AND CHEESE.

Quarter of a pound of Macaroni.
Half a pint of White Sauce.
Three ounces of grated Cheese.
Half a teaspoonful of made Mustard.

METHOD.

Break macaroni into 1 inch lengths, and cook in boiling salted water 20—30 minutes till soft. Make the white sauce, add macaroni and three quarters of the cheese and other seasonings. Turn into a greased dish, sprinkle the remainder of cheese on top and brown in a hot oven.

Macaroni Tomato. Substitute half tin of tomato soup in place of cheese, mix and bake as above.

BAKED EGGS.

For these, small baking dishes are required, *i.e.,* pyrex, casserole, or failing these small meat paste glass dishes may be used; or the eggs may be cooked together in one pie-dish. They may be served at table in the dishes in which they are cooked.

METHOD.

Grease each dish well, leaving about ½ teaspoonful butter in the bottom; add 1 tablespoonful milk to each dish, then break the egg into it. Place on a baking tray and bake in a moderate oven 5—10 minutes till set; eggs will puff up and look twice their size.

CREAMED EGGS.

Four hardboiled Eggs.
Half a pint of White Sauce.

METHOD.

Cut eggs in four lengthwise; make the sauce, put in eggs, heat thoroughly, serve on toast or on bed of mashed potatoes.

or

Chop the whites roughly and add to sauce; rub

the yolks through a sieve; pour the sauce over squares
of toast and sprinkle yolks on top, reheat.

ECONOMICAL BREAKFAST DISH.

One ounce of Butter.
Chopped Onion.
Remains of cooked white Meat.
One tablespoonful of Flour.
Half a teaspoonful of Curry Powder.

METHOD.

Melt butter in pan, add the onion and curry powder, fry slightly, add flour, mix together, cook for a
few minutes; add enough milk to make a smooth
thick sauce, season. Add the remains of any white meat
rabbit, chicken, etc., cut into neat pieces—or half cold
macaroni or rice. Reheat thoroughly. Dish neatly
and dust a little grated cheese on top. The addition of
a few sultanas is an improvement.

PEAS AND CHEESE.

One pound of marrowfat Peas.
Four ounces of Grated Cheese.
Half a pint of thick White Sauce.

METHOD.

Soak peas and cook according to directions on
packet, drain; grate cheese, add ¾ of it to sauce; when
thoroughly hot add peas, turn into piedish, sprinkle rest
of cheese on top; brown in oven.

A suitable accompaniment to the above is Baked

Potatoes.   Wash, peel potatoes, if big cut into half; make some dripping hot in a tin and bake until cooked and brown—about $\frac{1}{2}$—$\frac{3}{4}$ hour; baste and turn frequently.

TO USE UP STALE BREAD.
SAVOURY BREAD.

METHOD.

Cut up any scraps of bread into $\frac{1}{2}$ inch squares; put these into basin, pour over boiling water and pour off again.   Beat up an egg, add a cup of milk, salt, pepper, and mixed herbs; pour over bread in greased piedish, put pat of dripping on top, and bake in slow oven till hot and brown on top.   Serve in place of potatoes.

BREADCRUMBS.

METHOD.

Thoroughly dry in oven until a golden brown, crumbs and crusts of bread; crush with rolling pin on baking board or sheet of paper until quite fine, pass through a wire sieve.   Re-roll what remains, continue until all passes through sieve.   Keep in tin and use for coating foods for frying or baking.   Always re-sieve after use.

CINNAMON TOAST.

Four thin slices of Toast.
One teaspoonful of Cinnamon.
One teaspoonful of Sugar.

METHOD.

Toast the bread and butter while hot; mix cinnamon and sugar together and spread on top; cut into neat squares.

This is excellent for serving with afternoon tea.

MUSHROOMS.

To distinguish these from poisonous fungi, sprinkle a little salt on the gills; if they turn yellow they are poisonous; if black, wholesome. A silver spoon will turn black when used in cooking poisonous fungi; likewise a peeled onion. Never re-heat mushrooms; throw away all leftovers as they develop injurious properties. Mushrooms are found abundantly throughout Shetland; they form a wholesome food.

FRIED MUSHROOMS.

METHOD.

Wipe, remove stalk and peel; dip in egg and breadcrumbs and fry a golden brown in enough fat to almost cover.

STEWED MUSHROOMS.

METHOD.

Prepare as before, cut into neat pieces; stew in pan with a little milk and water and sliced onion for 15-20 minutes.

G

CREAMED MUSHROOMS.

METHOD.

Make 1 pint of White Sauce (see page 5).   Prepare mushrooms as before, add to sauce and simmer gently 15—20 minutes.

MINCEMEAT.

Quarter of a pound of Raisins.
Quarter of a pound of Sultanas.
Half a pound of Currants.
Half a pound of Apples.
Half a teaspoonful of Ginger.
Half a teaspoonful of Cinnamon.
Two ounces of brown Sugar.
Quarter of a pound of Suet.
Two ounces of Peel.
Half a teaspoonful of Nutmeg.
Quarter of a teaspoonful of mixed Spice.
One Lemon.   Pinch of Salt.

METHOD.

Stone and chop raisins; clean the other fruit; chop suet, apple and peel finely, grate lemon rind thinly. Mix all together with lemon juice; press into jars and cover until required.

DRESSED NEW   CABBAGE.

One new Cabbage.
Two Eggs.
One tablespoonful of Sugar.
Half a tablespoonful of Flour.
Half a teaspoonful of Salt.
Two and a half cupfuls of Water.
One ounce of Butter.
Half a cupful of Vinegar.

METHOD.

Cut cabbage in neat shreds. Break eggs into basin, add sugar, flour, salt and vinegar; mix well together, melt butter in pan, add mixture and stir slowly until it is cooked, about 5—10 minutes.; pour hot over cabbage, serve hot. (More or less vinegar may be added as desired).

Note.—This is a method of using uncooked cabbage.   It is quite digestible if cut in fine shreds, but the cabbage must be young.   It can also be cooked for 10 minutes in boiling salted water after shredding, and served hot with above dressing or a little butter.

BUTTER SCOTCH.

Two cupfuls of Sugar.
Vanilla.
Two tablespoonfuls of Water.
Two tablespoonfuls of Butter.

METHOD.

Boil without stirring until brittle when tested in

cold water.   Pour out on buttered plates to cool, and
mark in squares.

FUDGE.

Three cupfuls of Sugar.
One cupful of Milk or Cream.
One teaspoonful of Vanilla.
One tablespoonful of Butter.
Three or four tablespoonfuls of Cocoa or un-
    sweetened Chocolate.

METHOD.

Put sugar, milk and cocoa into saucepan ; stir and
boil until it makes a soft ball when tested in cold water.
Take from fire, add butter and vanilla, cool and stir
until creamy.   Pour on buttered plates and cut into
squares.   The addition of marshmallow whip is an
improvement.

BAKING POWDER.

Two ounces of Tartaric Acid.
Two ounces of Carbonate of Soda.
Two ounces of Rice Flour.

METHOD.

Roll tartaric acid with rolling pin till smooth.   Add
the other ingredients and roll until well mixed or pass
through a sieve.   Keep in a tin with a close fitting lid.

Preserves.

RHUBARB JAM.

Six pounds of Rhubarb.
Six pounds of Sugar.
One cupful of Water.
Two Lemons, or One pound of Figs, or
    Two ounces of Root Ginger.

METHOD.

Wash and dry rhubarb, cut into $\frac{1}{2}$ inch lengths; put into crock or basin, add sugar, a cup of water to start juice, and soak for 24 hours. Turn all into preserving pan and stir occasionally while coming to boil. Cut ginger into small pieces and add; or grate lemon rind and add with lemon juice; or soak figs overnight, cut into small pieces and add. Boil $\frac{1}{2}$—$\frac{3}{4}$ hour until jellied and thick. Dish in warm pots, and cover when cold. This will keep a year or longer.

MARMALADE

Three pounds of Seville Oranges.
Two Lemons.
One sweet Orange.
Nine pints of Water.
Six to Seven pounds of Sugar.

METHOD.

Wash and dry oranges, pare outside skin thinly and shed finely; put into basin, cover with water and soak for 24 hours.   Slice the whole oranges roughly, soak with measured water (3 pints to 1 lb.) in basin or crock for 24 hours.   Put into preserving pan and simmer gently for 2 hours, strain through cheese cloth; boil skins separately 2-2½ hours till soft; measure all liquid and allow 1 lb. sugar to 1 pint liquid, and 1 lb. sugar to 1 lb strips.   Return all to pan and boil quickly for ¾-1 hour till jellied.   This quantity will make 12-14 lb.

APRICOT   JAM.

Two pounds of dried Apricots.
Four pints of Water.
Two pounds of Apples.
Four pounds of Sugar.

METHOD.

Soak apricots in measured water overnight and cook next day in same water for 30 minutes or until thoroughly soft.   Wash, pare and slice apples and stew in a little water until quite soft; add these with sugar to apricots and boil quickly for 10—15 minutes until thick and jellied.   Dish in pots and cover.   This will keep for several weeks, but not for a long period.

INDEX.

88 INDEX.

ERRATA.—Page 27, line 8, read—

Note.—In certain districts when milk was, etc.